We are Procession, Seismograph

Devon Balwit

Nixes Mate Books
Allston, Massachusetts

Copyright © 2017 Devon Balwit

Book design by d'Entremont
Cover photograph from the collection of Lauren Leja

All rights reserved. This book or any portion thereof may not be reproduced or used in any manner whatsoever without the express written permission of the publisher except for the use of brief quotations in a book review or scholarly journal.

ISBN 978-0-9993971-4-5

Nixes Mate Books
POBox 1179
Allston, MA 02134
nixesmate.pub/books

Art belongs to everybody and nobody. Art belongs to all time and no time. Art belongs to those who create it and those who savor it. Art no more belongs to the People and the Party than it once belonged to the aristocracy and the patron. Art is the whisper of history, heard above the noise of time.

—Julian Barnes, THE NOISE OF TIME

Contents

Dawn Chorus	1
Caravan	2
Cabinet of Curiosities	3
Inward	4
Rotation	5
Prophet	6
As Usual	7
In the Swamp	9
Composition	10
Zeno's Paradox	11
Onkos I	12
Onkos II	13
Onkos III	14
Eclosion	15
Repulsion	16
I Box the Forms	17
Late in the Game	18
Ollie, Ollie, Ox in Free	19
Proof	20
Down There	21
What We Run From	22

Angels' Lament	23
Wrack Line	24
Deaf Ears	25
In Contrast	26
Though the Waters Thereof Rage and Swell	27
Experiment	28
Fukushima	29
Sortilege	30
Mary and Martha	31
From the Trenches	32
Triage	33
Resignation Syndrome (I)	34
In the Blue Forest	35
Crepuscule	36
(Pensive)	37
Sweetheart, Come	38
(Tenderly)	39
For those in the Audience	40
Study for the Whole	41
Evening Chorus	42

We are Procession, Seismograph

Dawn Chorus

Enter the dawn chorus. The swoop dive of grackles, the cooing of doves. I cock my head, fill the pitcher of my ear with busyness. All day, I will take tiny sips. Even myopic, I recognize the small belligerence of a hummingbird staking claim to an antenna. Snowy egrets progress across lavender hills. Of the rest, I am mostly ignorant. Still, I parse the score, staccato and sibilance, true to my nature.

Caravan

Our shadows show what we are. Even slantwise, they are truer. We are procession, seismograph, our pulse so quiet the night nurse, too, can doze. Our legs elongate like staves, the mode Maqam. Slowly, we advance over scouring, nictitating membranes a burnished shield. Our haunches undulate. We mesmerize those behind.

Cabinet of Curiosities

Daily, the needle unsugars the blood, the bridge restores the smile, the girdle grips. Nestled in velvet bags, bright chains tangle rivers. Stockings convolute a silken cerebrum. Gloves press, pray, pair. My own hands plunge, reading the braille of hooks and rough lace, the talc glissando. Flesh is mystery, pocked and pendulous. I piece it out. I try it on.

Inward

In the lobby, the piano awaits, tuned to caverns and bluffs. Its dark keys ready themselves, ravens testing wind, while its white keys shut eyelids against the coming glare. Footsteps patter all around, the piano untroubled by their current. Years away, someone approaches, fingers already in motion.

Rotation

The world spins me, tucked into its spokes, thoughts a gymnast's ribbon flaring, altered by degrees, wheeling through sun and shadow. I stretch, twist, pull tight, the maypole center of vast forces. Journeying, I am herm, wherever I stand, center. The light about me breaks color. I gather shards, pocket palettes. I toss fracture this way and that, sowing the jagged.

As Usual

...at the usual time, in the usual place...
           Steve Lacy

I turn up my collar against the weather but not the crumpled condom, the flung gust of someone's carfuck. Its rumple resurrects the Condom Man, champion of safe sex, who visited my classes with his condom pump, blowing up dozens at a time: French ticklers, ribbed, flavored, lubricated. Whenever he sensed attention's flag or embarrassment's creep, he'd pump it, pump it, pump it, like the upstairs neighbor's squeaky bed, and they'd inflate. No one could frown before this variegated porcupine, gaining and losing turgor. (The same cannot be said about his puzzling, dental dam, a talc-y non-starter, like cunnilingus at a drive-through carwash.) I'm not Proust and so must settle for discarded latex to take me back to my Combray, where clueless, chafing against the ordinary, I somehow let solipsism obscure the march of history – the Berlin wall crashing, the first Gulf War, Rodney King, the Oklahoma City bombing. It was hard, then, to get a sense of scale, like walking the Nazca lines. Up close, they seem mere scraped earth, while from hillcrest or higher, they morph into tarantulas, monkeys, geckos. To the present, I'm as blind as when I birdwatch, unable to pick feather from leaf, breeze from wing. Decades from now, something will tap everything into sudden focus, something ordinary.

Prophet

The lamp lifts two blind sockets from the trash. The cat on the sill knows I wonder if it works, but it reveals nothing as it licks paw pads. To carry around a lightless lamp weighs Biblical. I'm not sure I'm up for it, but I submit. Strangers queue up behind. I unlock my door and sling it in. Moments later, a faint glow cracks the blinds. The waiting crowd, taking this as a sign, falls prostrate.

In the Swamp

Sunset in cypress, water ripples a hot shimmer. I pole through the red pulse that pounds in my temples. A palimpsest of summers swallows me up, *perhaps* and *maybe*, spangled fish, leaping open-mouthed for flies. I drop a line, caring little whether barb snags boot or bream. Whatever surfaces, I will toss back.

Composition

Arching backwards, I wait for my partner, wind, to catch me beneath arms and swirl me, a compass needle. Ribbed, winged, hollow, I travel a great distance, my skull flaring flame. Aroused, I bleed, but in filaments, painterly. Embraced by negative space, neither male nor female, I answer need, entering and being entered. Over the throb at my throat, a single white feather pulses.

Zeno's Paradox

The fists, for now, find me. Trick is to let the pain explode outward, concussion's cloud cloaking ache. Time and again, scar-sutured, I reassemble. Dread regrows, but I tie it back, like hair. I refuse to believe the cat unfriendly, lower myself, dogged, to its claws. One day the blow won't fall, between it and me an infinity of half-ways.

Onkos I

Somewhere a tumor grows in mad metastasis, a garden gone riot. In me, even now, it spills its bed. My plans will keep their tight crease, my feet never leave the gangway. Incipient, words freeze, no next. Why me? Because I was fertile and ready to seed. Listen to the humming, the secret burgeoning. More until no more. No moral.

Onkos II

I dowse my body, searching for hidden springs. I cannot see, but sense them, bubbling deep. Quivering against my palms, the rod pulls. I call upon another to auscultate, to tap and to cap. Even so, the rod still trembles, knowing me a land of multiple fissures.

Onkos III

My waters run yellow, flooded and foul. I vomit over rocks. You are wise to hold the children back. One misstep and, they would go under. I know you would throw me a rope, but where am I? Already submerged. You can tell people that: *She was already submerged.* One look at where it happened, and they will believe you. No one could survive that.

Eclosion

I am chrysalis. Bright form geometric. Say *cremaster*. Say *metamorphosis*. Feel, as I do, the crack as tightness splits to unfurling. I cling where you never think to look. This my dun dwelling, this my makeshift. Not so after, when body's bellows spreads me bright. Then you do see and ready your nets.

Repulsion

Clickbait, the daypack's tag promises *100% Human Leather*, Steve McQueen's tattoos, his moles. Its pretty designer tells the camera our DNA floats free, unpatented, and can be netted. We lack exclusive rights, and so might come upon our skin someday refashioned—a tote bag, a pair of shoes. *Cool,* reads one reply, *I'd totally wear that.* I think of trophies from not so long ago, Black and Jewish scrotum sacks, lampshades, book covers, secret or not so secret heirlooms. Perhaps even cows cringe, recognizing the kin in skin. Leather. *I totally wear that.*

I Box the Forms

I box the forms, the parade of carbon rings to which hydrogen, nitrogen, and oxygen cling. The organic seems solid but lies, nothing more than protons and electrons vibrating mute attraction. I corral the molecular herd. I hem it in. Arc and cosine pick up megaphones. They shout over me. I tape them down, tape the tape, lock them into equations. I demand obedience to principle. Scornfully, they redistribute, associating with whichever one they please. They refuse binaries, squaring and negating. I put my hands over my ears. I put my head in a vise. I tighten the clamps until it threatens to split, a melon rind, a cervix crowning. I pocket each and every scrap. They writhe beneath my fingers in darkness, escape each time I remove my hands. I sew them in. Still they riot. You tell me – where do I go from here?

Late in the Game

It's midnight, but still the upstairs glows, an ectoplasmic pulse that signals the presence of my son. I can't tell you what he does, or only more or less, nothing as scurrilous as porn, but cooking shows, America's Got Talent. When not watching strangers animating ventriloquists' dummies, evading chainsaws, or pulling cards from the air, he's hard at work on his own skillset, narrowly defined, the epic win, being the last one standing in Battle Royale, breeching a fort in Rust, chock full of death-dealing materiel. I hover on the stairs debating if it's worth the climb. Regardless, he won't notice me, positioning himself intentionally out of sight, headphones in. It seems late in the game to admonish, but don't we always say that after giving up?

Ollie, Ollie, Ox in Free

Shoat, checkerboard, skate park. I grip the bridge as it lifts to hang me above dark water. I squeal when chased, sucking barked knuckles. Both our blood tastes the same. I massage my scalp where you dragged me by hair. *Stop*, I said, *don't*. Next time, greased, I'll slip through your fingers. I'll castle, entrench to my strongest square. I careen now, railslide, the grind good, roughing me smooth. I sacrifice, goofyfoot, less, more.

Proof

(for Adelaide Hall)

How sticky he is, stare-button eyes, crocheted cock. Cock and bull, they say, but I still feel him in me. The others, too, are there, snared, too small to do anything but cling, our mother dead. And the apple tree, slink-snaked, doves wise to secrets, but flying over. I've my own hook now, threat, threaded. Then, I had nothing but tooth and nail, easily overmastered. Call it lie, but I've woven it plain, the twist of it. Some families are like that, never picked, never to be unpicked.

Down There

The wind gusts my skirt. Panicky, I slap it down, fretting, *no panties, no panties,* remembering sitting spread-kneed on bleachers, a Girl Scout leader barking, *shut your legs!* as indignant as if I'd left a burner on, a faucet running. The cool current teases like skinny dipping, water slipping everywhere, the surprise as luscious as being five and masturbating, squeezing, squeezing, thinking *I could do this forever.*

What We Run From

The man rises from a shallow grave the way certain ideas do, refusing to settle to bone, not a monster although circumstances have conspired to make him one, filthy and half sutured. He crawls, then staggers, a procession slow and painful. We are not surprised when he cauterizes his own wounds with lit gunpowder, when he sinks his teeth into raw meat. He has proven himself ready to go the distance, comfort forgotten as he pursues justice, no joy awaiting the act, only grim satisfaction. So, too, certain ideas, left for dead, claw themselves up, leave blood trails in snow, sniff their way back to us by changes in the wind, by moss on bark, by the stars. We think we have ditched them, but they reappear – ruptures, mistakes – banging on our palisade. We run, but there is no evading them. Made for this, they are the ones that survive, somehow purified the more ragged they get, tracking us until we drown in gore, then float downstream to snag, battered by current.

Angels' Lament

We lift from skins abraded by mesa, by asphalt. Wrists twist into cuffs, then free, like plucked wings. We flap as we fall, blood spraying constellations. All around us, the surge of feet, sirens, the wind. Our mothers claw their way close and gather us up. They unfold us in memory until we split at the seams. Our fragments mound altars, eyelids reddened by votives. We say we are coming. We whisper all that we know. Perhaps we, only, can hear.

Wrack Line

The suicide runs, always just out of reach. *Tell me*, I say. I want to listen. Or. *Enough*, I say. I've heard enough. The days repeat themselves, a semaphore of want, a dark stoop of talon, piercing. Ankle deep, I wade through the remains. My ears recoil like spent shells on shingle. *Shh*, they say. *Shh*.

Deaf Ears

Your invisible rays shock, so I ground myself with silver boxers, wear conductive socks. You doubt me even though you don't doubt the lake, reflecting while the unseen flails beneath. And what of the family portraits seemingly undisturbed by the scrabbling and squeaking deep in the walls? You've always been happiest surrounded by mirrors, pain bright. Why would I make this up?

In Contrast

Seated on the Buddha's toenail, I am tiny. I fold over my ticking like the case of a watch dangling from its chain. How patient the lichen. How understanding the bodhisattva of all that collects in his cracked places, the patina of lowliness. In contrast, I am roil, cloud-scudding across the swaddled void. It's all I can do to remain for an instant. The Buddha keeps still, and will keep so, forever.

Though the Waters Thereof Rage and Swell
(after Psalm 46)

How patiently the horse stands, water rising all around, barn reduced by a third, paddock nothing but post tips. From what used to be hillock, it watches the world melt away. The bloated sow and her piglets floating. The bobbing sheep. Murk parts left and right about its broad chest. Hungry, it endures hunger. Sodden, it endures wet. There, slips the farmgirl, appleless, ribbons trailing. And next the farmwife, apron amuck. The horse whickers and flares its nostrils, still, awaiting the farmer.

Experiment

The monkey has taken the baby, borrowed its mother's dress. How sweetly it rocks what it hasn't eaten, what remains of love. Both are pinked with pleasure as the larger croons, pouring its heart into its dear ribbed bowl. *My littlest love, my darling. Join me in canopy, together to clamor, together to groom.* After a time, baby's silence disheartens. The monkey disrobes and swaddles its stillness. It curls baby back into cradle. Once again fur only, it hoots and bares teeth, lifting a parting arm, hieratic.

Fukushima

The empty town runs with boars, cells lifting Cesium lanterns as they scavenge. Their eyes glow in the unpeopled corridors. Ratpacks join them, nightgrass skittering claws. Cytosine unspools from guanine, adenine from thiamine, then rewinds, dabbling. In the clamor of Geiger counters, hunters shy away. Carcasses mound, uneaten, unburned. Marginal, the animals' own edges fray; beetles sport puzzle-box elytra, lizards creep on stubs. The strange beasts root and multiply, sheltered by the long half-life of human error.

Sortilege

The universe tosses its horns, each hoof clattering comets, new dimensions. White-rimmed nebulae snort and champ. I am both here and not yet. A flocking of stars, a molecular burnish. A far-flung door sucks back curtains. I pull the corolla round, threading black holes as light breaks, shushing, on sky shingles. Geometries cavort along axes. What the final form? Take each from me like a cat's cradle. Keep it taut, the better to balance on threads.

Mary and Martha

You feather-tickle away the day while I strap myself tight. Belt upon belt, past the last hole, to where buckle bites skin. You laugh, skirt breeze-gusted, sunlight always saving itself for you, honey in the comb. Lips pursed, I pinch shadows. Streak rivulets, fog glass. You pay me no mind, your head ringing carillon. Bright, bright. I squint to take you in.

From the Trenches

The cold sings to us over the throb of our wounds, a melody difficult to resist. It slips its hands beneath our clothes and caresses. We can feel ourselves harden although we wish it were otherwise. Even our tears freeze, stalactites of grief. Our last letters crinkle against us as we writhe, whispering, as at our funeral. We want to scratch some mark into the stones beneath our cheek, our final resting place, but we have nothing but our nails, fungal and soft. We only bleed. Already, the hungry ground swallows us up. We shout *mother, mother* in a vast fugue, voices all around. This is the best we can do, this composition of gore.

Triage

The interred claw themselves from dirt. Exotics curl comatose or reach through the bars of small cages, limbs straining. Clumsy from shock, the exsanguinating scoop blood into the sieve of their bodies two-handed. Tears streak a child's cheek dust. An earless dog cowers. A cat's neck seeps in a too-tight collar. The blood-spatter of family wrings a man before plumed smoke. Dazed, the living hold up their pain. I dash from one to the next, stunned by need, while more mound, hourglass ever-spilling.

Resignation Syndrome (I)

We trail longing, swaybacked and chafed from everything we can't put down. Scavenging transit points like bones, we crack them at night for their marrow, sucking out the embryonic, the never-will-be. Our eyes rime with the faces of strangers, hard-eyed stares that wish us gone. Soon, we are gone and going further, war-flooded through gutters, swirling, pushed from behind. Each time we snag, we are rent, flapping from branches. Lips move all around. We watch them from an uncrossable distance, wills winked out, even the smoke-curls scattering.

In the Blue Forest

The forest shrinks to fence slats, wears to grain. It snags clouds in its jags, guts them for showers. I peer through to a cellular landscape, golden, busy. Stretching my arms, I spin. Distance catches me dizzy. The slats mumble like old men sagged into story, a saga of wind. A knot is a nose is an eye is a ring. Reaching, my cupped palms catch light while shadows gather deep in the cracks. When the sun bruises, I take refuge between ridges, folding into dark like a blanket.

Crepuscule

I lift the gangway behind me, seeking distance from the day, a cabin so small that when I stretch out my arms, I touch walls in all directions. I want rocking. To orient by leeward and starboard, fore and aft, the compass rose, the stars. Climbing to crow's nest, I guzzle featureless horizon. Nothing breaks but weather, the briefest apparition of fin and feather. Like a babe at the shoulder, I nestle into rigging. Woven into sky, I sing, accompanied by wind-blasted sails. *Yes to the swell. Yes to the waterspout. Yes to the shrouded dead tossed to scavengers.* There is no feed, only feeding, the invisible roil beneath, nothing caustic beyond salt rime. Already, I am becoming a ghost ship. I bleach and buckle. I sag beneath barnacles.

(Pensive)

Pensive, I hold both light and shadow, pass from I to I as on stepping stones across mirrored water. Not inert, I wheel and orbit the flare of my own dwarf star. One hand tuck and grooves between my lips. The other curves to catch a breast ripe enough to fall, all of me, pendant, composed as any tombstone, any orator, briefly lit, darkness ringing me round.

Sweetheart, Come

she writes, come, come. The doors are barred against me. Time is a chained goldfinch pacing its perch. Sweetheart, come. We used to segment a ripe pear, placing an end in each our mouths and meeting in the middle. Remember? Now, I am ripe. I am segmented. Where are you? Sweetheart, come. Undo my restraints, untangle my hair, lift me from my fecal bed. The paper they give me is never enough. I cross it in waves, break against its edges, but find myself still here. Still. Here. I retreat in a sucking of shingle, a grinding. Sweetheart, come. With each pass of the pencil, I scratch a spell. I shape you in grey scale, hoping that, when the lead wears to blood, you will appear.

(Tenderly)

Tenderly, roseate, she stands amidst steer carcass wings. Split vertebrae, fascia, fat, lift delicate lace behind her cameo face. She pities me as I drink in beauteous slaughter. Her full breasts and round belly call eye and hand. I wonder if she is cold, how her nostrils do not flare at the charnel. Disgusted, I cannot look away. *I know*, she seems to say. *Such a fine line between horror and beauty.*

(after a photo by Nicola Constantino)

For those in the Audience

Look up. On a tightrope, anyone can walk, but I pedal. The crank arm blurs. My body centers, then centers again, tipping through multiple plains. Down below, your faces reflect light like feeding fish, mouths agape. Your Icarus, you want me both to arrive at the far platform and fall. You ready a collective gasp, hunching against the imagined weight of me. I don't blame you. It's what we're here for, that giddy sway at the edge of plummet.

(after Francis Bacon's, Portrait of George Dyer Riding a Bicycle, *1966)*

Study for the Whole

I piece myself together, stitches raw, borrow arms to juggle limbs, tightrope teetering. *Glyph*, I say, *Wild hair*. The winning spermatozoa has changed his mind, but his tail only drives him deeper in. He will have to love his blossoming cage. Forever after, he dreams of exit signs, blinking. *Tic tac toe, a dog, a tombstone*, all he will ever need. I pat him on the back. I commiserate. I remain to the end, his best, his dearest friend.

Evening Chorus

The hills funnel shadows onto the jacarandas, Scriabin bruising the silence. With equal passion but less grace, neighbor dogs join in. In its mountainous bowl, the town sets, the details of the day stiffening. Birdsong flares in flung handfuls, grackles and flycatchers returning to roost. Trucks appear and disappear like needles along the ring road's hem, distant vibrations from elsewhere.

Acknowledgments

Eclosion | *Sooth Swarm Journal*
Experiment | *Noble/Gas Quarterly*
Fukushima | *Smeuse*
I Box the Forms | *Cordite*
In the Blue Forest | *The Inflectionist Review*
Lifelike | *Posit*
Mary & Martha | *Sweet Tree Review*
(Pensive) | *Allegro*
(Tenderly) | *Yes Poetry*
Rotation | *Cease, Cows*
Sortilege | *Noble/Gas Quarterly*
Ollie, Ollie, Ox in Free | *taplit magazine*
Sweetheart, Come | *taplit magazine*
Wrack Line | *taplit magazine*
Composition | *Menacing Hedges*
From the Trenches | *Menacing Hedges*
Proof | *Menacing Hedges*
Triage | *Menacing Hedges*

About the Author

Devon Balwit teaches in Portland, OR. She is a poetry editor for *Minute Magazine* and has seven chapbooks and one full-length collection out or forthcoming: *How the Blessed Travel* (Maverick Duck Press); *Forms Most Marvelous* (dancing girl press); *In Front of the Elements* (Grey Borders Books), *Where You Were Going Never Was* (Grey Borders Books); *The Bow Must Bear the Brunt* (Red Flag Poetry); *Risk Being/ Complicated* (self-published with the Canadian artist Lorette Luzajic). Her full-length collection, *Motes at Play in the Halls of Light* will be published by Kelsay Books in 2018. Her individual poems can be found in *Cordite, The Cincinnati Review, The Carolina Quarterly, Fifth Wednesday, The Stillwater Review, Red Earth Review, The Fourth River, The Free State Review, Posit*, and more.

Nixes Mate Books features small-batch artisanal literature, created by writers that use all 26 letters of the alphabet and then some, honing their craft the time-honored way: one line at a time.

More Nixes Mate titles:
ON BROAD SOUND | Rusty Barnes
KINKY KEEPS THE HOUSE CLEAN | Mari Deweese
SQUALL LINE ON THE HORIZON | Pris Campbell
COMES TO THIS | Jeff Weddle
HITCHHIKING BEATITUDES | Michael McInnis
AIR & OTHER STORIES | Lauren Leja
WAITING FOR AN ANSWER | Heather Sullivan
A WORLD WHERE | Paul Brookes
MY SOUTHERN CHILDHOOD | Pris Campbell
THE WILLOW HOWL | Lisa Brognano
CAPP ROAD | Matt Borczon
NIXES MATE REVIEW ANTHOLOGY 2016/17
HEART OF THE BROKEN WORLD | Jeff Weddle
STARLAND | Jessica Purdy
SMOKEY OF THE MIGRAINES | Michael McInnis

Forthcoming titles from Nixes Mate:
LUBBOCK ELECTRIC | Anne Elezabeth Pluto
JESUS IN THE GHOST ROOM | Rusty Barnes
SHE NEEDS THAT EDGE | Paul Brookes
LABOR | Lisa DeSiro
A FIRE WITHOUT LIGHT | Darren C. Demaree
THE LIFE OF ATOMS | Lee Okan
HE WAS A GOOD FATHER | Mark Borczon

nixesmate.pub/books